# LIFT THE FLAP
# Nativity

WRITTEN BY
**Juliet David**

ILLUSTRATED BY
**Gemma Denham**

**CANDLE
BOOKS**

Mary looks surprised and happy.
**_Lift the flap to find out why._**
An angel is visiting.
"You will have a very special
baby," he says.

Mary and Joseph are snug in the stable.
They are very happy.
**_Lift the flap to find out why._**
Baby Jesus has been born.

These shepherds look very startled.
What are they staring at?
*Lift the flap to find out.*
The angels say: "Go to Bethlehem to find baby Jesus."

The wise men are kneeling in front of Jesus.

*Open the door to find out how the men journeyed here.*

*Lift the flap to see what gifts they brought.*

Gold, frankincense and myrrh.

*LIFT THE FLAP NATIVITY*

Copyright © 2007 Lion Hudson plc/
Tim Dowley Associates
All rights reserved.

Written by Juliet David
Illustrated by Gemma Denham

Published in 2007 by Candle Books
(a publishing imprint of Lion Hudson plc).

Distributed in the UK by Marston Book Services Ltd,
PO Box 269, Abingdon, Oxon OX14 4YN
Distributed in the USA by Kregel Publications,
Grand Rapids, Michigan 49501

Worldwide co-edition organised and produced by
Lion Hudson plc, Wilkinson House
Jordan Hill Road, Oxford
OX2 8DR England
Tel: +44 (0) 1865 302750
Fax: +44 (0) 1865 302757
Email: coed@lionhudson.com
www.lionhudson.com

ISBN 978 1 85985 684 0 (UK)
ISBN 978 0 8254 7342 5 (USA)

Printed in Malaysia